GW00454965

PRAYERS TO START MY DAY

DAVID O'MALLEY SDB

Don Bosco Publications
Thornleigh House, Sharples Park

Bolton
BL1 6PQ
www.don-bosco-publications.co.uk
01204 308811

All readings based on Scripture
have been paraphrased,
references are given
as indication of source.

ISBN 978-0-9555-6548-9

Don Bosco Publications
Thornleigh House
Bolton BL1 6PQ
Tel 01204 308 811
Fax 01204 306 868

www.don-bosco-publications.co.uk

Email joyce@salesians.org.uk

Other books by DAVID O'MALLEY
Swatch & Pray
School Ethos & Chaplaincy
The Christian Teacher
Christian Leadership
Ordinary Ways
Prayers to Close My Day
Trust the Road
Via Lucis

Printed by Buxton Press Limited

Contents

Benedictus

Blessed be the Lord
who comes today to set us free.
Our liberation has arrived
from within our own experience.
We have been set free from frustration
as the prophets had foretold.
God's promises have been fulfilled
and we are sanctified.
For there is a Child given to us
to be with us on the road.
God's tender mercy, like the morning sun,
rolls back the darkness of our lives.
We walk with God, out of the shadow of death,
side-by-side, in the way of peace.
Glory be to the Father and to the Son
and to the Holy Spirit.

Our Father

Our Father who art in heaven,
hallowed be Thy name;
Thy kingdom come;
Thy will be done on earth,
as it is in heaven.
Give us this day our daily bread;
and forgive us our trespasses,
as we forgive those who trespass against us;
and lead us not into temptation,
but deliver us from evil. Amen

Introduction

Morning and Evening Prayer are the two hinges on which the Prayer of the Church turns. The reflection on life, alongside the words of scripture, has been a daily practice in the Church since earliest times. This book continues that tradition, offering a simple form of prayer for individual or communal use at the start of the day.

The structure of the prayer is simple. It begins with **The Sign of the Cross** and a **Greeting**. An **Offering** of the day is made, with a brief pause. The **Scripture** is said slowly, and where two or more are gathered, it can be said by alternating voices. A brief **Meditation** is provided each day, to be read quietly or read aloud in groups. There is then a chance to reflect on **The Day Ahead** in the light of scripture, followed by a brief pause.

The Benedictus and **The Lord's Prayer** are included each day, as a link to the traditional Office of the Church. **The Final Prayer** has been based on the official Prayers of the Church for each Sunday of the year. Finally there is a phrase –**To be repeated often during the day**. This can easily be remembered, and repeated like a mantra, linking us back to the prayer that started our day. The language throughout the book has been adapted to make it immediately available to those of us who may not have a strong background in regular prayer and scripture reading.

This book is presented as a partner volume to,

Prayers to Close My Day.

It is offered as a way of prayer for busy people. It is also offered as a resource to Christian communities who would like to start their day with a simple form of prayer. It is also presented as an occasional alternative to the full Office of the Church for religious communities and parishes.

Sunday – Week One

In the name of the Father, and of the Son, and of the Holy Spirit.

Peace be in this new day, peace of heart and mind.
Peace with the past, peace with the future.

Pause

May the peace of Christ make a home in my heart.
May it disarm anger and calm all fear today.
May it settle in my soul and stay.

Offering

Lord, I offer you this day,
with all the promise and uncertainty it contains.
I offer you all my fears and hopes for the day.
Be the peace at the centre of my life today.
Be the hope that survives each event.
Be with me in all that happens.

Scripture

Based on John 20:19

It was Sunday and the doors were closed in fear,
when Jesus came and stood among his disciples.

Jesus gave them peace to calm their fears
and showed them his wounded hands and feet.

Peace be with you Jesus said again,
calling them into the way of Risen Life.

Jesus breathed on them.
The Spirit moved in their hearts,
the Spirit of peace and new beginnings.

Happy are those who have not seen,
yet clearly see with the eyes of faith.

Glory be to the Father and to the Son
and to the Holy Spirit.

Meditation

We live for only six hundred and fifty thousand hours.
Like a morning mist,
our individual lives seem to come and go,
with little importance and much frustration.
But peace becomes possible when we remember
that the morning mist of our lives is the breath of God.
We are caught up into God's own life,
not just as individuals,
but as an inspired people,
at the heart of history.
All will be well.

The Day Ahead

Where will peace be felt strongly today?
What thoughts will keep me focussed and peaceful?
Where am I at risk of losing my peace of mind?
To which situations and people
do I need to bring peace?

Pause

Benedictus & Our Father *see page 4.*

Final Prayer

*Let us pray that Christ's peace
will find a welcome in the day ahead.*
Father, let your family likeness grow in us today.
Deepen the Spirit of Jesus in all we do.
Send us into a world
of fragile peace and broken promises,
as signs of hope and of Gospel joy.
Touch our hearts again in the hours ahead,
turning them to thoughts of peace. Amen

To be repeated often during the day
Peace I leave with you.

Monday – Week One

**In the name of the Father, and of the Son,
and of the Holy Spirit.**

Greeting
One thing I ask of God; this is all I need,
to live in God's presence, every moment of this day.

Pause
May I seek God's face,
and recognise the goodness of God,
on the journey of this day.

Offering
Father of creation, I offer you this new day of my life.
Walk with me through all that will happen.
Open my ears to hear your voice guiding my steps.
May I walk in a Gospel path and come home tonight,
with your will done, your Kingdom built up
and our friendship forever deepened.

Scripture
Based on Psalm 1:1-3
Blessed are those who do not walk in bitterness,
who turn their steps away from anger and pessimism.

Blessed are those who search out God's presence,
who uncover the law of love, day and night.

They are like trees planted by flowing waters,
they will never become hard-hearted or withered in spirit.

They will not be blown about by misfortune,
but stay faithfully rooted in God's goodness.

Whatever they do will be drawn into God's wise plan.
The fruit of their lives will last forever.

Glory be to the Father and to the Son
and to the Holy Spirit.

Meditation

Our life-journey unfolds in mystery, each moment is a gift.
Sometimes our day is littered with failure and frustration.
Sometimes success and surprises overwhelm us with delight.
The way of the Christian disciple challenges us
to accept both these experiences, as gifts from God.
We are called to love and trust
both the Cross and the Resurrection,
as part of the wisdom of God,
who calls us all to be sons and daughters.

The Day Ahead

Does the shadow of the Cross
darken any part of the day ahead?
Where is the light of Resurrection
likely to shine on my path today?
What challenges do I need to talk to God about,
as the day begins?
Where will I find it hard
to retain a sense of God's presence?

Pause

Benedictus & Our Father *see page 4.*

Final Prayer

Let us pray for peace as this day begins.
Ever-present Father, your watchful care surrounds us.
You organise creation,
so that even the tensions and tragedies of sin
never frustrate your loving plans,
to bring everything to Resurrection.
Help me to embrace your will today,
give me strength to follow your call.
Let your truth live in my heart,
to reflect peace on all I will meet on today's journey. Amen

To be repeated often during the day
Lord, stay with me on the journey.

Tuesday – Week One

In the name of the Father, and of the Son, and of the Holy Spirit.

Glory be to God for the gift of this new day.
Glory be to God for light and life.
Glory be to God for time to learn and grow in love.

Pause

Lord, teach me to trust your providence.
Guide my thoughts and actions,
to accept the gift of this new day with hope.

Offering

Lord, I offer you this day,
in which your heart and mine can share all that happens.
I offer you all my hopes for this day,
and all the frailty that I bring to life.
Speak to my heart, in its strength and its weakness.
Help me to build your Kingdom, of love and justice,
in the hours that lie ahead.

Scripture

Based on Ezekiel 34

I will become the shepherd of my sheep says the Lord,
I will seek out the lost and the hidden.

I will rescue them from unhealthy places,
to bring them home to their own land.

When they are scattered by the storm,
I will gather them together in safety.

I will collect the strays and heal the hurt,
I will build up the weak, and guide the strong.

For you are my own flock,
I am your Shepherd.

Glory be to the Father and to the Son
and to the Holy Spirit.

Meditation

Each day we are shepherded through experiences,
both new and old.
Like sheep we can follow the crowd
and lose touch with the Shepherd,
wandering into darkness and danger,
without the support of a wise guide.

As followers of Jesus,
we are invited to listen
for the voice of the Good Shepherd in our hearts.
We are challenged to trust that voice,
even when the way leads
beyond the understanding of our mind or heart.

The Day Ahead

Where will I hear the voice of the Good Shepherd today?
What will stop me from hearing God's voice?
What dangers lie ahead today, for my peace of mind?
What do I need to ask of God as the day begins?

Pause

Benedictus & Our Father *see page 4.*

Final Prayer

Let us pray for God's guidance in our hearts
Lord, the love you offer draws us beyond ourselves.
A love exceeding the deepest desires of our hearts,
for you are greater than the human heart.
Guide each thought and action of the day ahead,
so that our frailty and faults
may not hide your presence,
but lead us into your providence and peace. Amen

To be repeated often during the day

The Lord is My Shepherd.

Wednesday – Week One

**In the name of the Father, and of the Son,
and of the Holy Spirit.**

Save us, Lord, from cold hearts
and from closed minds,
as a new day begins.

Pause

Open us to your love.
May we touch eternity today,
hidden in our ordinary lives.

Offering

Lord, I offer you the journey I make today.
May it be woven into your eternal plan of love
for all creation.
Let me walk alongside others,
my eyes wide open to the way your love
links our journeys together.

Scripture

Based on Isaiah 43

The Lord says, *Do not be afraid, you are my people.*
We belong together, I have named each one of you.

When you are out of your depth, I am still with you.
When the waters are rough you will not sink.

Because I am God, you cannot sink beyond my care.
I will always sustain you on the journey of life.

So do not be afraid, I am with you each day.
I will gather all that has been scattered.

I will bring you home to the heart of God.
I made you to be with me forever.

Glory be to the Father and to the Son
and to the Holy Spirit.

Meditation
In the Christian tradition
God calls each person individually,
but each person is also called into relationship with others.
We go to God together.

The people of God travel through time,
uncovering the mystery of God's presence in their world,
handing that mystery on to future generations.
It is a shared journey,
into the presence of God at the heart of creation.
This morning we begin another stage on that journey.

The Day Ahead
With whom will I share the journey of this day?
Who will bring me closer to God today?
Who will need my support to get through the day?
How am I called to live out the Gospel today?

Pause

Benedictus & Our Father *see page 4.*

Final Prayer
*Let us pray for a greater love of people,
made in God's image.*
Father, from the days of Abraham
until this morning,
you have gathered people together,
and shared your presence with them.
Bless your people on this new morning.
May we keep learning how to love each other,
even as you have loved each one of us.
May your love support us whatever we find
in the day that lies ahead. Amen

To be repeated often during the day
Do not be afraid for I am with you.

Thursday – Week One

In the name of the Father, and of the Son, and of the Holy Spirit.

Greeting
Lord of this morning hour,
Father of light and strength,
today I bring you my poverty and need.

Pause
Come into my emptiness.
Use my weakness as well as my gifts.
Be a companion through this new day.

Offering
Lord, I offer you this day and all that it will bring.
Anchor my day deeply in your presence.
Steady my heart and mind,
when emotions within and challenges without,
threaten my peace of mind.
Take this day and let your will be done.

Scripture
Based on Jeremiah 31
The people that fled into the desert
have found God's friendship.

Looking for a way to escape
they discovered God, searching for them.

So they began to love their God again,
building their lives around God's presence.

They were met by God with an everlasting love,
an unchanging affection for God's faithful.

In that love they rebuilt their lives together.
Instead of grumbling, they began to sing.

Glory be to the Father and to the Son
and to the Holy Spirit.

Meditation

I want it and I want it now
has become a mantra of our culture.
We are impatient with waiting and emptiness,
suspicious of stillness,
uncomfortable with silence.

Yet, when we are driven
into the desert of our own emptiness;
we find a God who is always searching for us.
In that silence, we find that the depth of our emptiness
is simply the echo of a love that never ends.

The Day Ahead

Where will I feel most vulnerable during the day?
What will drive me into the empty silence within me?
When will I feel most impatient today?
Where will God be searching for me,
in the hours ahead?

Pause

Benedictus & Our Father *see page 4.*

Final Prayer

Let us pray to be patient with our weakness.
Lord, you know every thought in every mind.
No joy or tear goes unnoticed by your loving care.
Watch over us at the start of a new day.
Remind us of the power we have to love,
and the poverty of our spirit.
Open to us today
the hidden treasures of your Kingdom. Amen

To be repeated often during the day

Blessed are the poor in spirit.

Friday – Week One

In the name of the Father, and of the Son, and of the Holy Spirit.

Greeting
God loved us so much that he sent his own Son,
to be with us in the challenges of today.

Pause
Lord stay with us in your wisdom.
May this day bring us closer to you,
and to each other, in your Kingdom.

Offering
Lord of wisdom, I offer you this day,
with all my hard-won wisdom and experience.
I offer you the uncertainties and confusion I face today.
I offer my mixed motives, my fears and my selfishness.
Send your wisdom into all my thoughts, words and actions,
so that I may become an instrument of peace,
a source of strength for others, in your wise hands.
Let your wisdom work in my weakness.

Scripture
Based on Wisdom 9

Lord, all wisdom comes from you,
wisdom beyond understanding.

Send that wisdom into our lives,
to help us and work with us today.

May wisdom guide our choices,
protecting us from folly in our plans.
Lord, none of us can understand your plans.

We need to trust your wisdom.
It is only in You, that we can learn wisdom,
through your Spirit that has been sent into our lives.

Glory be to the Father and to the Son
and to the Holy Spirit.

Meditation

The life and death of Jesus reveal a wisdom,
that challenges our view of success and failure.
It is a wisdom that often reaches success through failure,
a Risen Presence that grows stronger in our weakness.

When we look at our work and relationships,
the same wisdom becomes a challenge of faith.
There is a wise purpose working within our weakness
– God's wisdom of the Cross.

The Day Ahead

Where do I need to ask for God's wisdom today?
How am I likely to experience my weakness,
during this day?
Who are the wisdom-figures in my life today?
What successes can I look for today?

Pause

Benedictus & Our Father *see page 4.*

Final Prayer

Let us pray for the wisdom that goes beyond words.
Father, in Jesus your wise plan
became flesh and blood.
Becoming one like us,
Jesus has changed our human story,
into a relationship of love
with a wise and creative God.
As our story unfolds into a perfect love,
help us to trust the Gospel wisdom,
in the life of the Risen Jesus,
who waits for us
at the start of this new day. Amen

To be repeated often during the day
God chooses what is weak, to shame the mighty.

Saturday – Week One

In the name of the Father, and of the Son, and of the Holy Spirit.

God of shyness and subtlety,
thank you for being with me this morning.
Uncover your presence in this new day.

Pause

Open me, heart and soul, to your Kingdom.
May I hear your word,
sifted into the sounds and silences of this day.

Offering

Lord, thank you for all the anticipation and anxiety,
with which I meet this morning.
I offer you every thought, word, event and each encounter.
May they all find meaning and depth in your presence.
Let the work I do today
be helpful, in your plan, for a better world.

Scripture

Based on Luke 13:18

What is the Kingdom like, to what can I compare it?
It is like a small mustard seed thrown onto the ground.
It becomes a tree, in which the birds can shelter.
The Kingdom of God is like a pinch of yeast,
transforming plain flour into risen bread,
to feed deep and hidden hungers.
Don't always take the easy way out of problems.
Enter by the narrow door.
Stay focussed on the hidden life of the Kingdom.
Do not let yourselves be separated from God,
nor locked out of the celebration of the Kingdom.
Do not let your love of God become a thing of the past.
Glory be to the Father and to the Son
and to the Holy Spirit.

Meditation

The Christian path leads, through loss and failure,
towards new life.
It is a path that is hidden,
from the clever and the calculating.
It is open only to the trusting and child-like spirit.
The road to the Kingdom is easily overlooked,
in the challenges of the day.
It is the path towards self-sacrifice,
liberating honesty, fragile faith
and self-emptying generosity.
The path lies hidden in the day ahead,
if we have eyes to see the way.

The Day Ahead

What would make this day successful for me as a Christian?
What blind spots could put me at odds with God's Kingdom?
Is there a hidden place in my day, to find God's presence?
Where will I cross God's path, in other people today?

Pause

Benedictus & Our Father *see page 4.*

Final Prayer

Let us pray for hope in God's goodness.
Father of all people,
trusting your word is the path to wisdom.
To search for your word is to grow in truth.
Open our eyes to your presence,
in creation and in community.
Open our ears to your call in the day ahead,
so that everything we choose will lead us deeper
into the hidden life you offer your children. Amen

To be repeated often during the day

The Kingdom of God is among you.

Sunday – Week Two

In the name of the Father, and of the Son, and of the Holy Spirit.

Greeting

Thanks be to God for life and breath,
for strength to trust, for a will to love.

Pause

Open my mind and heart Lord
to all the gifts that lie in wait,
along the journey of this day.

Offering

Lord, I make a gift of this day to you.
Use my time, my energy and thoughts as you will.
I place my life in your hands, to use as you wish.
Whether this day holds humiliation or success,
I offer it all, as a small part of your loving plan
for the transformation of creation.

Scripture

Based on Matthew 7:13

Don't always take the easy way.
There are no short-cuts to God.

Try to enter by the narrow way of self-denial,
by the hard road of committed trust in God.

Be slow to trust others, as guides for the journey.
Judge them by what they are, not by what they say.

It is not those who have the right words that matter,
but the ones who do the Father's will.

Those who listen and follow the Father's will,
build their lives on an eternal foundation.

Glory be to the Father and to the Son
and to the Holy Spirit.

Meditation

God asks simply that we do our best,
in living a spiritual life.
When we have planted and watered let us not forget
that it is God alone who can make things grow.

For that reason we need to learn
to wait on the providence of God.
If we seem to be making no progress at all,
let us maintain our peace of mind.
Let us leave the abundance of the harvest to the Lord.

St Francis de Sales

The Day Ahead

What expectations do I bring to the day?
Are these expectations worthy of me and realistic?
How will I trust in God's providence today?
How will I choose the narrow and challenging path today?

Benedictus & Our Father *see page 4.*

Pause

Final Prayer

Let us pray for trust in God.

Father, open our eyes to everyday blessings.
Deepen our trust in your constant presence in life.
May friendship with you become the foundation
of an eternal relationship with all creation.
Bring us closer to your Kingdom
of justice and peace today. Amen

To be repeated often during the day
I place all my hope in you Lord.

Monday – Week Two

**In the name of the Father, and of the Son,
and of the Holy Spirit.**

Greeting

Thanks be to God for creation and new life.
Thanks be to God for time to grow and change.
Thanks be to God ever old and ever new.

Pause

Father thank you for a new day,
for all its uncertainty and routine patterns,
it is the place where you and I will work together.

Offering

Lord, I offer you my life today,
with its mixed motives and plans for the hours ahead.
Take my heart and purify my motives.
Take my mind and clarify my plans.
Make me a good and faithful servant of your Kingdom,
in all that happens.

Scripture

Based on Luke 16:10

The one who is trusted in little things
will be trusted with greater responsibility.

The one who is dishonest in small things
will never be trusted with what really matters.

If people cannot be trusted with ordinary things,
who would trust them with genuine riches?

No one can satisfy the demands of two masters,
you cannot be the slave of both God and money.

It is too easy to act the part of a virtuous person.
God reads the heart and knows the truth about us all.

Glory be to the Father and to the Son
and to the Holy Spirit.

Meditation

The inner spirit is never free
from the outer culture in which it lives.
There is a daily tension
between the demands of an outer world of the possible,
and the demands of an inner world of hopes and ideals.
The first can lead to superficiality,
the second to unrealistic hope and disappointment.

The Gospel liberates us
from both disappointment and superficiality,
by putting a relationship with the Father,
at the centre of each life.
This relationship grows deeper,
as it meets disappointment and emptiness.
This relationship is the way of the Cross.

The Day Ahead

How will I be tempted to serve another god today?
What motives lie behind my plans for the day?
Where do I need to challenge other values today?
Where will I deepen my relationship with God?

Pause

Benedictus & Our Father *see page 4.*

Final Prayer

Let us pray to the God of freedom and new life.
Father, words cannot contain the mystery of your love.
Lift us beyond the limitations of measured lives,
to the eternal reach of your loving kindness,
uncovered in the Death and Resurrection of Jesus.
Set us free to live and love in the same Spirit,
that moved Jesus to give his life for others. Amen

To be repeated often during the day

Lord, you know my heart and my mind.

Tuesday – Week Two

**In the name of the Father, and of the Son,
and of the Holy Spirit.**

Lord of life and love,
thank you for this new day,
gifted to us by your kindness.

Pause
Lord of challenge and change,
stay with us in all that happens,
in the day that lies ahead.

Offering
Lord, I offer you this day with all the generosity I have.
I give you each hour, each decision and each challenge.
Help me to choose the path of love today.
Whether it be in compassion or in challenge,
may I learn to do the most loving thing.
May I ease the pain and injustice of the world
and help to build your Kingdom today.

Scripture
Based on Luke 6:25
Love your enemies.
Do good to those who hurt you.
Bless those who curse you.
Pray for those who treat you badly.
Give to everyone who asks.
Do not chase the one who robs you.
Treat others as you would wish to be treated.
You will be children of Our Father in heaven.
Love your enemies, do good to those who hurt you.
Your reward will be great in heaven.

Glory be to the Father and to the Son
and to the Holy Spirit.

Meditation

Personal fulfilment is not part of the Gospel message.
The Gospel is about recognising God's presence,
and doing God's will,
in generous self-sacrificing love.

Christians certainly need to develop their personal gifts,
but the motivation is not self-fulfilment,
but self-emptying.
The love that liberates is not self-love,
but the love that dares to give meaning to death,
by growing through emptiness,
into an eternal relationship with God.

The Day Ahead

What patterns of selfishness
will I tend to slip into today?
Where will I be called upon
to turn the other cheek?
Where will my generosity be tested?
Who are my enemies today?

Pause

Benedictus & Our Father *see page 4.*

Final Prayer

Let us pray for the strength that comes from God's love.
Father, we thank you for the trust that binds us together,
aware that selfishness can tear us apart.
Keep us united in the love
that gives meaning to our lives.
Help us to draw encouragement
from the Gospel we follow. Amen

To be repeated often during the day
Love your enemies.

Wednesday – Week Two
In the name of the Father, and of the Son, and of the Holy Spirit.

Father of Creation,
thank you for this newly created day,
to be shared in your presence.

Pause
Father, may I be with you today,
as fully as you move in my heart and mind,
at the beginning of this new day.

Lord, I offer you today the air that I breathe,
the water I wash with, and my energy to move in your world.
Keep me open to the way your presence is moving in my day.
Like air and water help me to bring freshness and inspiration
to all the challenges I meet today.

Based on Luke 12:35-40
Be dressed and ready to get into action.
Don't let the darkness cloud your mind.
Be like a doorkeeper,
waiting to open up when the master comes home.

If you are ready to welcome the master,
you will be treated as a friend and companion.

Those who stay awake will recognise danger
and not allow violence to enter their home.

Stand ready and be watchful.
The Lord will come at a time you do not expect.

Glory be to the Father and to the Son
and to the Holy Spirit.

God's love cannot be contained,
because it is alive
and flowing through all life.
We become aware of this flow,
when we listen with the heart,
for what is life-giving.

Then, like a doorkeeper,
we can open our lives
to an eternal love flowing in time.

The Day Ahead

How do I feel as I begin this day?
Am I ready to be sensitive and flexible today?
Where am I in touch with life and energy this morning?
What attitudes and memories
may block my life and love today?

Pause

Benedictus & Our Father *see page 4.*

Final Prayer

Let us pray to the Father whose love keeps us safe.
Lord, help us to recognise you
as the source of creation,
a loving Father
at the heart of each person.
Teach us to cling to your promises
in an uncertain world.
Keep us safe in your peace and secure in your love,
as we share your work of creation today. Amen

To be repeated often during the day

Lord, let your love flow through me today.

Thursday – Week Two

**In the name of the Father, and of the Son,
and of the Holy Spirit.**

Greeting

Thank you Lord for the dawn of a new day,
for the gift of light and life.
Thank you for vision and purpose to guide my steps.

Pause

Lord of light stay with me today.
Enlighten my doubts and desires.
Shine through my choices today.

Offering

Lord, I offer you my hopes and fears today.
I offer you the light and shadows within me.
Let me walk in the light of your presence all day.
May your light shine through me clearly that others will
recognise your goodness in me.
May I never hide your light in the way I live today.

Scripture

Based on Matthew 6:22

The eye opens the whole body to the light.
Good eyesight fills a person with light.
A damaged eye will bring shadows and uncertainty,
filling a life with darkness.
If the light within a person becomes dark
how can that person ever trust what they see?
How is it that you can see a splinter in another's eye,
and ignore a plank in your own?
Do not judge and you will not be judged.
Because the judgements you hand out
will be the ones you receive yourself.
Glory be to the Father and to the Son
and to the Holy Spirit.

Meditation

We are called to be children of the light,
– open, playful, honest
and dependent upon God.
Darkness creeps into our lives when we forget to play,
when we choose isolation
and take ourselves too seriously as independent people.

We are not made for independence.
We are made to belong to a loving Father.
We are children of the light, not of darkness.
Our hearts are restless,
until we recognise our dependence on God.

The Day Ahead

What shadows are there inside me as the day begins?
Where will lightness and truth be most accessible today?
Who will need the light of my presence today?
Where will I find darkness a threat?

Pause

Benedictus & Our Father *see page 4.*

Final Prayer

Let us pray for strength to turn away from darkness.
Father of all creation,
in Jesus, your light has broken into our lives.
Through the Cross and Resurrection,
your love has been uncovered
as the heart of the universe.
Guide us by that Gospel light today.
Lighten our hearts with your truth today. Amen

To be repeated often during the day
The Lord is my light.

Friday – Week Two
In the name of the Father, and of the Son, and of the Holy Spirit.

Lord, open my mind and heart this morning,
to see the world through your eyes,
to act as you would wish throughout this day.

Pause

Help me to speak the truth in kindness,
to admit my mistakes honestly,
and give my time generously in this new day.

Offering

Lord, I offer you this unused day. I offer all the enthusiasm
but also the reluctance I feel for what lies ahead.
Be with me in my fears, to calm my mind.
Be with me in success and surprises, to help me celebrate.
Be with me in the silence, to deepen my love for you today.

Scripture

Based on Luke 12:1

Be on your guard against hypocrisy,
for everything that is hidden,
will eventually be uncovered.
What you have said in secret,
will be said in the light of day.
What you have whispered quietly,
will be shouted out loud.
Do not fear what can only harm the body
fear instead what can harm your friendship with God.
No one is beyond God's friendship and loving kindness.
Every hair of your head has been counted.
Even a sparrow is not forgotten in God's sight.
You are worth much more than sparrows.
Glory be to the Father and to the Son
and to the Holy Spirit.

Meditation

As a Christian,
I do not need to fill my life with noise,
busyness or many people.
At times it is good to stop,
and let the dust of activity settle –
to know what I will find in the silence.
At first there may be some disappointment and restlessness,
but beneath, there is more –
gratitude for life itself,
humour at my own silliness,
compassion for suffering in life
and a quiet wisdom,
distilled from a spirit-filled life.
God's truth is never far away.

The Day Ahead

Where will I find it hard to be honest today?
How will I find space for stillness?
Do I feel that I am worth more than many sparrows?
How will I be a sign of God's loving kindness for others?

Pause

Benedictus & Our Father *see page 4.*

Final Prayer

Let us pray for enthusiasm in serving others
Father, in the Resurrection of your Son,
death became a doorway to new life.
His courage and faith have opened up a new age of hope.
Let us never drift back into old ways,
or be content with empty promises and short-lived success.
Keep us close to you today, make our happiness holy,
and all our love, life-giving for others. Amen

To be repeated often during the day

The truth will set you free.

Saturday – Week Two

**In the name of the Father, and of the Son,
and of the Holy Spirit.**

Thank you Lord, for another opportunity,
a chance to live another day in your presence,
a chance to share your life with others.

Pause

Thank you Lord for your word,
sown in my heart and history.
May it find deeper roots in my life today.

Offering

Lord, I offer you my life and all my understanding.
I offer my anxiety, distractions
and everything I value in the day that lies ahead.
Let your word take root in my fragile life.
Through my actions, may your word produce wisdom
and kindness, to be broken open and shared
with all those I meet today.

Scripture

Based on Matthew 13:18

Those who hear the word without understanding
find that word carried away from their hearts.
Those who allow the word little depth in their lives
soon find that it is uprooted in time of trouble.
Those who receive the word without trust
allow anxiety and worry to stifle its goodness.
Those who do not welcome the word as a treasure
are likely to devalue it in their daily living.
Those who hear, welcome and act on the word
produce a rich harvest of life and truth
for many people.

Glory be to the Father and to the Son
and to the Holy Spirit.

Meditation

If you really want to reach God
and want that desire summarised in just one little word,
here is your answer:
the word is **Love**.

Fasten this word firmly to your heart,
so that it never leaves you.
Whatever befalls you, cling to this word in your heart.
If any other thoughts press themselves upon you
to ask what you want or need,
you have the answer in this little word,
Love.

The Cloud of Unknowing
14th Century English Mystic.

The Day Ahead

What distractions might lie ahead for me today?
Where will cares and worries stifle a sense of God's presence?
Where will I be able to draw on experience and wisdom?
Where will I find depth and stillness today?

Pause

Benedictus & Our Father *see page 4.*

Final Prayer

Let us pray that we will be faithful
to the light we have received.
Father, surrounded as we are by uncertainty,
let the light of your truth
guide us deeper into your Kingdom today.
Help us to trust the Gospel you have given to us.
Let your love form us all into the family
you have called us to be. Amen

To be repeated often during the day

The harvest is great and labourers few.

Sunday – Week Three

In the name of the Father, and of the Son, and of the Holy Spirit.

Greeting

Thank you Lord, for this morning,
for the fading stars and the rising sun,
calling me back into action in your world.

Pause

Thank you for another chance
to share in the mystery of your life-giving love
at the heart of creation.

Offering

Lord, I offer you my heart today.
May I remain in touch with my feelings
and in touch with you.
Show me the road that leads deeper
into the story of Cross and Resurrection.
Help me to recognise your invitations
to share in your self-sacrificing love for others.

Scripture

Based on Matthew 20:17

We are travelling towards Jerusalem,
to the city of the Cross and Resurrection.
To a place of rejection, mockery and death,
towards struggle, and conflict with authority.
You know that authority usually makes itself felt;
it likes to maintain its own greatness.
If you want to be great you should become a servant.
Only then will you grow into the Kingdom of God.
The Son of Man came not to be waited upon,
but to pour out his life in the service of many people.

Glory be to the Father and to the Son
and to the Holy Spirit.

Meditation

When we move the focus of our lives
from our own needs to the needs of others,
a liberation is achieved.
A force is set free inside us
that can transform lives.
That force is genuine love,
and for those who receive it, unmistakable.

When we want possessions,
people or knowledge,
just for ourselves,
we block the flow of love and compassion in the world
and everyone suffers as a result.

The Day Ahead

How do I feel about the day ahead?
Where do I feel empty, where do I feel enriched?
How will I use the power of love and compassion today?
How will I handle authority today?

Pause

Benedictus & Our Father *see page 4.*

Final Prayer

*Let us pray for an increase in compassion
in the human heart.*
Lord, let the goodness of your life continue to grow in us.
Draw us deeper into the life-giving process of change.
Teach us the wisdom of the Cross and Resurrection.
Help us to overcome injury and injustice.
Increase our compassion for those who suffer. Amen

To be repeated often during the day
Greatness comes through service.

Monday – Week Three

In the name of the Father, and of the Son, and of the Holy Spirit.

Greeting

Lord, thank you for the touch of your hand,
waking me from sleep,
helping me to start the day.

Pause

Thank you for my frailty and needs,
leading me to rely more on you,
than on my own independence.

Offering

Lord, I offer you this day
and invite you to share it with me.
Touch my day with your hand.
Guide all my actions, my thoughts and my feelings.
May I recognise each touch of your hand today.
Give me the trust and the courage to respond,
when you invite me into action or to stillness.

Scripture

Based on Matthew 18:1

Who is most important in God's Kingdom?
The one who becomes as open and trusting as a child.
Unless you change and become like a child
you will not be able to grow into God's Kingdom.
Whoever recognises their own frailty and needs
will be most important in God's eyes.
Those who realise and welcome their dependence
welcome God's presence into their lives.
Those who avoid their own frailty and emptiness
will also miss God in their experience.
Glory be to the Father and to the Son
and to the Holy Spirit.

Meditation

The basic characteristic of childhood is dependence,
finding strength in others and relying upon it.
As Christians we are called to dependence,
to a kind of vulnerability to others and to God.
A vulnerability which is life-giving.

Independence is not our natural state.
We are made for one another,
to search out the meaning of life and love,
together with other people.
The image of the child reminds us
that our frailty and dependence
are vital signposts on the path to truth and life.

The Day Ahead

Who will I be happy to depend upon today?
Where will I resent being dependent?
Who will need to depend upon me today?
When will I find time, like a child, to play?

Pause

Benedictus & Our Father *see page 4.*

Final Prayer

Let us pray for the gift of recognising God's presence
Lord, open our eyes
to see you in the beauty of creation,
and in the mystery of each fragile human life.
This world is holy because it is touched by your hand.

Touch our lives this morning with your loving kindness,
so that we can share this day with each other,
in self-giving and service. Amen

To be repeated often during the day
Whoever welcomes a child, in my name, welcomes me.

Tuesday – Week Three

**In the name of the Father, and of the Son,
and of the Holy Spirit.**

Lord, thank you for finding me,
in these quiet moments,
before I begin the day.

Pause

Help me to find you
and recognise you, calling my name
in today's rhythms and routines.

Lord, I offer you my day.
Help me to see the paths and pitfalls that lie ahead.
Be with me, as a shepherd, guide and protect me every hour.
Open my ears to your call to do what is loving and wise.
Give me the courage to recognise and accept
the help you offer on the day's journey.
Make me ready to support others,
in your way of love today.

Based on Matthew 18:12

A shepherd owned one hundred sheep
and one of them was lost.
He left the ninety-nine safe in the fold
and went to find the stray.
The shepherd found more delight in the stray
than in the ninety-nine who never left the fold.
As it was with the shepherd in the hills
so it is with Jesus, the Shepherd of our souls.
Jesus delights in bringing to the Father
those who are far from their home.
Glory be to the Father and to the Son
and to the Holy Spirit.

Meditation

Our culture is more concerned with productivity
than community.
There is a temptation to busyness rather than being.
Our self-worth is tied too closely to achievement,
rather than to our dignity as human beings.

For Christians,
those who are weak,
under-achieving, dependent, difficult,
become graced signs of a deeper dignity.
Their needs remind us of our own frailty,
they call us home to a more honest relationship
with God and one another.

The Day Ahead

To what am I likely to close my ears today?
What kind of distractions will I have to manage today?
Where will my patience be challenged today?
How will I find time to listen for God's word?

Pause

Benedictus & Our Father *see page 4.*

Final Prayer

Let us pray for a kindness that never fails.
Lord, you shower us with gifts each day.
Each life is an eternal gift from your love.
Shepherd our lives in your loving kindness today,
for only your love can make us whole and bring us home.
May the generous sharing of our gifts and needs
reveal your path of love in the day ahead. Amen

To be repeated often during the day
I am the Good Shepherd I know my sheep.

Wednesday – Week Three

**In the name of the Father, and of the Son,
and of the Holy Spirit.**

Thank you God, for all that will happen today,
for all the surprises and sameness,
that will make this day unique.

Pause

Thank you for gathering up each event
and drawing it into your plan
of Cross and Resurrection to new life.

Offering
Lord, I offer you my day,
my unique experience of your life and love.
Take this day and my reactions to all that happens.
Help me to co-operate with your inspirations,
and shoulder the crosses that come to me,
on the way to a deeper love for life and people today.

Scripture
Based on Matthew 25:34

Come to me you who have been blessed by my Father.
Receive the Kingdom for which you were made.
For I was starving and you gave me food
I was thirsty and you gave me a drink.
I was a refugee and you made space for me
I was naked and you clothed me.
I was sick and you nursed me
in prison and you visited me.
Lord, when did we see you thirsty or naked?
When did we see you a refugee or in prison?
In so far as you helped any of my brothers and sisters
you helped me, says the Lord.
Glory be to the Father and to the Son
and to the Holy Spirit.

Meditation

The birds of the air have a nest
to escape to, in their need.
A stag has a thicket to hide in,
to avoid being caught by heat or by hunters.
So our own hearts need a place
to escape to, briefly, during the day.

It may be a picture of the Cross,
or an image of the wounds of Christ,
which put our struggles
into a wider context of purpose and meaning.
There is a strength and wisdom in this kind of practice.

St Francis de Sales

The Day Ahead

In whom will I find it easy to see God's goodness today?
In whom will it be difficult to see God's goodness?
When will I need to escape and be still for a short time?
What cross do I need to shoulder today?

Pause

Benedictus & Our Father *see page 4.*

Final Prayer

*Let us pray to be signs and bearers
of God's love for others.*
Father, renew us in spirit this morning.
Touch our lives again with your presence, living in people.
Help us to grow in your family likeness.
May we share your goodness
with our brothers and sisters, wherever we meet them
during this newly-created day. Amen

To be repeated often during the day
I was hungry and you gave me food.

Thursday – Week Three

**In the name of the Father, and of the Son,
and of the Holy Spirit.**

Risen Lord, you breakfasted by the lake
with your disciples.
Be with me, as I start my day.

Pause

In ordinary moments, in meals and in meetings,
may I recognise your Risen Presence.

Lord, I offer you this day.
Help me live out your challenge to love You,
and my neighbour, in everything that happens.
Give me a glimpse of your goodness in creation
and in the words and faces of all those I meet
in the day ahead.

Based on Mark 12:28
The first commandment is this
There is one God of all creation
who is to be loved with heart and soul and strength.
The second commandment is this
You must love one another
with as much strength as you love yourself.
To love God with heart, understanding and strength
is more important than rituals and detailed rules.
To love your neighbour as you love yourself
is more important than any pious prayers.
Those who live these words in their lives
are close to the Kingdom of God.
Glory be to the Father and to the Son
and to the Holy Spirit.

Meditation

It is so easy to claw back or compartmentalise
our Christian commitment.
We become selective about our love of God
and our love of our neighbour.
In doing this, prejudice and self interest
undermine the generosity
of our first commitment to the Gospel.
It is easy to smuggle back into our hearts
the values of a selfish world.

Each day is a challenge to recommit ourselves
to radical service of God and neighbour.
I must be ready to start again today.

The Day Ahead

How will I show love for my neighbour today?
During this day, when will I find space for God?
How will I show respect for myself and others today?
Who, in my circle of awareness, needs my prayer and help?

Pause

Benedictus & Our Father *see page 4.*

Final Prayer

Let us pray humbly and hopefully before our God.
Loving Father, your love goes beyond all boundaries.
Your care embraces the whole of creation.
May the barriers of prejudice
and the abyss of ignorance that divides us
be bridged by your love and goodness,
living in ordinary people. Amen

To be repeated often during the day
Love your neighbour as yourself.

Friday – Week Three

**In the name of the Father, and of the Son,
and of the Holy Spirit.**

Greeting

Thank you Lord for the hours that lie ahead,
whatever they hold.
I know I will share them all with you.

Pause

Thank you Lord, for the partnership we live each day.
I will find strength to do the right thing
and, in that sharing, a truth that lasts forever.

Offering

Lord, here is my day.
I gather all my thoughts about the day ahead,
my hopes and fears, and I put them in your hands.
May I reach out for your hand in peace and in panic.
May we meet the day together,
so that I can grow in love and honesty with others.

Scripture

Based on Mark 4:35

Leaving the crowd, Jesus got into a boat with his disciples.
A great storm began to threaten their crossing.

Jesus was alone in the stern, tired-out with work.
His head was on a cushion, he was fast asleep.

The disciples, in frantic fear, woke him.
They were amazed at his calmness in the fierce storm.

Jesus woke up. He spoke to the wind and the sea.
A great calm settled around them.

Jesus asked the disciples to rise above their fears,
through trusting their Father in heaven.

Glory be to the Father and to the Son
and to the Holy Spirit.

Meditation
Lord, you refused to answer,
when Pilate asked you, *What is truth?*

The truth is not just facts,
but relationships and meanings.
Each experience in life is an unfolded truth,
a part of the pattern of meaning and relationships,
that leads us deeper into our own lives and purpose.

The truth is not something we can get hold of.
You are the Truth, who takes hold of us,
and makes us sons and daughters of God.

The Day Ahead
What aspect of truth do I need to focus on today?
What storms of life do I anticipate in the day ahead?
What memories will help and hinder my plans today?
How will I renew my trust in God throughout the day?

Pause
Benedictus & Our Father *see page 4.*

Final Prayer
Let us pray for truth and integrity in our lives.
Lord, you are the source of all truth.
Everything comes together in your plan for life.
Help us to hear your word in every sound we hear.
Help us be patient, as your truth emerges in our lives.
In all the uncertainties of a changing world,
help us to cling to you, Lord,
more than to life itself. Amen

To be repeated often during the day
Why are you afraid, where is your faith?

Saturday – Week Three

**In the name of the Father, and of the Son,
and of the Holy Spirit.**

Lord of inspiration move in my life today.
Help me do your will.

Pause

Lord of peace and forgiveness,
be with me to build bridges,
to forget the pain of the past.

Lord, I offer you this day with all it may bring.
I offer you my awareness of your presence.
Let it grow deeper today.
I offer you the fears that come from past failure.
Help me to distil wisdom from experience.
I offer you my trials and temptations.
May they bring me closer to you today.

Based on Mark 1:9

Jesus came from Nazareth to the river Jordan.
He was baptised in the river by John.

The skies were torn open above Jesus.
The Spirit descended on him, in the form of a dove.

This is my beloved Son, a voice declared from heaven.
My love and friendship rests on all he does.

The same Spirit drove Jesus into the desert,
to be alone and to be tested for forty days.

Jesus was with the wild beasts
and angels looked after him.

Glory be to the Father and to the Son
and to the Holy Spirit.

Meditation

Many people think that because they feel bad,
God is far away and unhappy with them.
They assume that God is only interested
in happy and successful people.
In fact God is with us in all our moods.

We believe in a Gospel
that recognises the importance of failure,
isolation, suffering and even death,
as key points in finding a deeper relationship with God.
God slips through the cracks in our emotional lives,
to deepen a relationship that will heal us and last forever.

The Day Ahead

Do I feel God's favour rests upon me this morning?
What moods seem to isolate me from God's presence?
Where will I be tested in the day ahead?
Where will I be invited into quietness today?

Pause

Benedictus & Our Father *see page 4.*

Final Prayer

*Let us pray to the God who forgives
and gives new life.*

Lord, source of everything that is good,
give us the will to please you in the day ahead.
Open our minds to the ways your love works,
so that we might become wise in our weakness,
and grow stronger in trusting you today. Amen

To be repeated often during the day

I am God's beloved.

Sunday – Week Four

**In the name of the Father, and of the Son,
and of the Holy Spirit.**

Peace in this morning light.
Peace to all those I will meet today,
Peace to anyone I will think about today.

Pause

Lord I accept the gift of this day with a peaceful heart.
Help me to keep peaceful in mind and heart,
whatever happens.

Offering

Lord, I offer you today the power I have to love others.
Make my love balanced and generous.
Help me to be fair and honest, but also kind and forgiving,
in the way I express care and concern.
Make this day another lesson in loving like you,
with generosity, justice and mercy.

Scripture

Based on 1 John 4:7

Let us love one another,
because love comes from God.
Everyone who loves with generosity
is already caught up into the love of God.
God has made the first move in this love,
sending Jesus to close the gap between God and humanity.
Since God has come close to us in love
we should love each other and overcome our differences.
No one has ever seen God,
but if we live in love we share God's own Spirit.
Everyone who lives a loving life
lives in God and God in them.
Glory be to the Father and to the Son
and to the Holy Spirit.

Meditation

The love that we see in Jesus
is full of warmth and concern,
his heart went out to people very easily.
But it was also a love that challenged,
courageously naming hypocrisy
and refusing to be manipulated by others.

It was a love in which justice and mercy met,
in a liberating and disturbing way.
This is the kind of generous, trusting love
that is the model for all Christian relationships.

The Day Ahead

Am I beginning this day at peace?
Where am I challenged by justice today?
Where will my heart go out to others in compassion today?
Where will I need to make the first move in mercy or justice?

Pause

Benedictus & Our Father *see page 4.*

Final Prayer

Let us pray for justice and mercy in our world.
Lord, in you, mercy and justice have embraced.
You have created us out of love.
Every day you draw us into the eternal circle of your life.
Help us to share our lives in both mercy and justice,
so that we may not be hard-hearted.
Challenge us to grow
in the discipline of your self-giving love. Amen

To be repeated often during the day
Love comes from God.

Monday – Week Four

In the name of the Father, and of the Son, and of the Holy Spirit.

Greeting
Thank you for the dawn of a new day,
the birth of new hope,
the beginning of a new chapter in God's love.

Pause
May I breathe in the newness of today
and breathe out those habits of mind and heart,
that diminish my power to love others.

Offering
Lord, I offer you my day,
balanced between the person I was yesterday
and the person I wish to be today.
Help me to keep growing in awareness of you,
and not cling to fears and false dreams.
Make this day a step towards the freedom of a heart,
renewed in the service of others.

Scripture
Based on John 14:23
If you love me, you will become like me.
The Father will make a home in your heart.
The Spirit will teach you everything,
keeping the Gospel alive in your actions.
Peace I leave with you,
peace that comes from trusting the Father.
Do not be anxious or afraid.
We are only separated for a short time.
I am going to join the Father
I shall return and take you with me.
Glory be to the Father and to the Son
and to the Holy Spirit.

Meditation

Poverty of spirit and simplicity of heart
are often undervalued in modern culture.
Being streetwise and self-contained
are much more highly prized.
But simplicity often cuts through the confusion of life
to peacefulness of heart.
Poverty of spirit leads to a mutual dependence,
that can enrich relationships.

Remembering our need can make us free in spirit
and able to love others as Christ loves us.
God chooses what is weak and foolish
to confound our plans and bring us back to love.

The Day Ahead

Am I open to learning from what might happen today?
Can I recognise my needs, as opportunities to trust?
Where will I find the peace that Christ promised?
How can I live as a daughter or son of God today?

Pause

Benedictus & Our Father *see page 4.*

Final Prayer

Let us pray for peaceful and dependent hearts.
Father, help us to trust that you are with us,
in the muddle and confusion of our lives,
May we recognise our poverty today.
Give us a simple heart.
Teach us to look after one another peacefully.
Keep us focussed on the call to serve as Jesus did.
May we learn to be true sons and daughters
of Our Father in heaven. Amen

To be repeated often during the day

Do not be anxious or afraid.

Tuesday – Week Four

**In the name of the Father, and of the Son,
and of the Holy Spirit.**

Greeting

Lord of the morning,
give me life and energy,
to begin this day well.

Pause

Take my strength and weakness.
Let it become a witness today,
to your hidden presence in our world.

Offering

Lord, I offer you my strength,
to use in witnessing to the Gospel today.
I offer you my weakness, to give me a deeper trust
in your presence in my life.
I offer you all the opportunities
I will have to challenge attitudes
that do not lead to your love and compassion for all people.

Scripture

Based on John 15:18

If the world rejected me it will also reject you too,
because we do not belong to this kind of world.
If you did belong to the world as it is today
you would be happy with its injustice and coldness.
But because I have called you out of that world
you will be at odds with it and a challenge to it every day.
I tell you this so that you will not be disturbed by troubles
and be ready to stand for the love that brings life.
I will send you the Spirit
to confirm and strengthen your witness to the Gospel.

Glory be to the Father and to the Son
and to the Holy Spirit.

Meditation

The radical nature of the Gospel is often weakened
by repetition in church,
and compromises in Christian action.
Loving enemies, sharing property,
the closeness of God and the dignity of each person,
all these put Christians
at odds with aspects of our present culture.

There should be a struggle going on each day,
between Christians and the world they live in.
I am called to continue that struggle today.

The Day Ahead

Where do I need to stand my ground today?
Do I see anger as a possible call to action from God?
What aspects of my world am I at odds with, today?
How do I recognise the Spirit in my own life experience?

Pause

Benedictus & Our Father see page 4.

Final Prayer

Let us pray for a love-based law in our world.
Father, justice is only perfected when founded on love.
Help us to deal with each other lovingly today,
even when we are hurt or angry.
May we act with justice,
and not let revenge affect our choices.
Help us support a law of love
that names and challenges
all that is not just
in our relationships and in society. Amen

To be repeated often during the day
Stand for the love that brings life.

Wednesday – Week Four

**In the name of the Father, and of the Son,
and of the Holy Spirit.**

Thank you Lord, for another day of experience.
May I never take for granted this gift of time,
to learn and love in your world.

Pause
Thank you for the lessons this day will bring,
the opportunity to know myself better
and recognise your presence.

Lord, I offer you all the words
that will cross my mind and my lips today.
May they be truthful, tactful
and touched with your creative love.
Use my words and actions
to add to the amount of loving kindness in the world.
Make me ready to work to build a better world.

Based on John 1
From the beginning there was the Word.
The Word was with God, the Word was God.
Everything that exists
came to be through the Word
and was marked with the Word's own life.
That life of God's Word
is the light of all people.
The Word was the true light,
that revealed the human heart and mind.
It is a light that overcomes darkness,
enlightening the hearts and minds of all people.
Glory be to the Father and to the Son
and to the Holy Spirit.

Meditation

Our God is a God of history,
present in and through what happens.
The daily struggles between friends,
the political squabbles of governments
and the search for knowledge are all areas
where God's presence and plans are at work.

The Kingdom, described in the Gospel,
emerges through ordinary events,
not in a separate sacred space.
Our God gets involved actively in the world through us.
We are called again to that partnership today.

The Day Ahead

Where do I need light in the day ahead?
Who needs my forgiveness today?
Where is God calling me
to partnership for the Kingdom today?
Where will my hope and trust feel most fragile today?

Pause

Benedictus & Our Father *see page 4.*

Final Prayer

Let us pray for the peace of the Kingdom.
Father, you give us time to learn from experience,
and begin each day a little wiser in your love.
Help us to extend this forgiving love to others today,
so that we might build our relationships on hope
and trust in your Kingdom among us.
May the beauty of this forgiving love
unfold in us today. Amen

To be repeated often during the day

I am the light of the world.

Thursday – Week Four

**In the name of the Father, and of the Son,
and of the Holy Spirit.**

Lord thank you for my life today.
Thank you for my body and mind,
my gifts and my story so far.

Pause

Thank you for revealing your presence
in the flesh and blood of Jesus.
Reveal your life in my flesh and blood today.

Offering

Lord, I offer you my body,
with all its strengths, aches and pains.
I offer you my mind
and the dreams and hopes it contains.
Take my life today, body and soul.
Let it become
a sign of your presence in the world.

Scripture

Based on John 1

The Word was made flesh in this world
and was not recognised.
The Word entered the world
and was rejected by God's own people.
But all, who could accept the Word,
found that they were children of God.
The Word became flesh like us
and lived alongside us.
We saw the grace of God's presence
revealed in flesh and blood.

Glory be to the Father and to the Son
and to the Holy Spirit.

Meditation

Many Christians see the flesh
as a dangerous source of temptation and weakness.
They are right, at least in part.
But the Gospel suggests that the flesh
is also the place where we meet God.
In the passion, and the fragility of our flesh,
God breaks into our lives.

In human compassion for each others' weakness
we also touch the forgiveness of God.
In the passion of the flesh
we touch the joy and energy of a creator God.
So, in the Gospel,
our flesh has been transformed through faith,
into a pathway to God's presence.

The Day Ahead

How does my body feel about a new day?
Am I taking care of myself in both body and soul?
Who needs my energy and passion today?
Where is gentleness and compassion needed today?

Pause

Benedictus & Our Father *see page 4.*

Final Prayer

Let us pray for courage to live the questions of life.
Father, the mystery of your presence overwhelms us.
Your goodness is beyond the touch of our hearts.
Your strength escapes the reach of our minds.
Give us courage to seek the mystery of your presence,
in the experience of living and the intuitions of faith. Amen

To be repeated often during the day
The Word was made flesh.

Friday – Week Four

In the name of the Father, and of the Son, and of the Holy Spirit.

Thanks be to God for life,
for it's mystery unfolding in time,
for it's meaning in my own story.

Pause

Thanks be to God for the chance to serve,
to grow in wisdom today, to love with a sincere heart.

Lord I offer you this new day.
I offer you my plans,
knowing that they might go wrong in many ways.
Stay with me during the day
help me to adapt and change my plans,
according to your plan of love and justice.
Help me to live this day with a sincere and sensitive heart.

Based on 1 Thessalonians 5:12

Be at peace among yourselves.
Give encouragement and strength to one another.

Warn those who are lazy and show care for the weak.
Give courage to the worried, be patient with everyone.

Don't let arguments linger on.
Don't let them spill over into revenge and coldness.

Try to do what is best for others in family and friends.
Strive to be happy and cheerful every day.

Turn your mind and heart to God's presence regularly.
Give thanks for all that happens.
Glory be to the Father and to the Son
and to the Holy Spirit.

Meditation

In our rush to achieve more,
we may be blinded by ingratitude
to what has already been achieved.
A grateful heart recognises and names goodness,
wherever it is found.
What we take for granted slips through our hands.
What we take for granted in ourselves,
may be lost as a source of grace.

There is a God-given energy in gratitude
that is part of the rhythm of each day.
We need to be thankful for the start of this day.

The Day Ahead

Where will I need to be most positive and grateful today?
How will loving kindness touch my day?
How will I serve others?
How will I allow others to care for me?
Where am I likely to make a fool of myself?

Pause

Benedictus & Our Father *see page 4.*

Final Prayer

Let us pray for sincerity of heart.
Lord, you catch each moment of our day.
In loving kindness, you give meaning to every event.
Travel with us on the journey of this day.
Support us in doing good.
Protect us from foolishness.
Help us to share your loving kindness
by a life of sincere service to others. Amen

To be repeated often during the day

Give thanks for all that happens.

Saturday – Week Four

In the name of the Father, and of the Son, and of the Holy Spirit.

Greeting

Father of creation, open my eyes to a new day,
to your presence hidden within this new beginning.

Pause

Take away the anxious fears that linger.
Give me courage to hope and strength to love.

Offering

Lord, I offer you my day.
I offer you the fears that sometimes haunt my heart.
May my fear become an opportunity
to trust you more and learn my limitations.
Open my eyes to the ways
in which you turn a challenge into a new chance,
and a failure into faithfulness.
Help me to live this day in the logic of your love.

Scripture

Based on Romans 8:14

Everyone who is moved, in heart or mind, by the Spirit
is a daughter or a son of God.

This is not a spirit of slavery or manipulation.
It is a spirit of free choice, inherited by God's own children.

The whole of creation shares this journey towards freedom.
It aches and groans in waiting to be set free.

The Spirit comes to help us, in our waiting weakness,
connecting us to God, in a way deeper than words.

God lives with each person in love.
God turns everything to their eternal good.
Glory be to the Father and to the Son
and to the Holy Spirit.

Meditation

We are, as Christians, a Resurrection people.
We believe that tombs are temporary resting places.
But we can live a very different reality,
in our daily thoughts and plans.
We tell ourselves that we will never overcome
some problem or issue.
We tell ourselves that some people
are beyond help or forgiveness.
While we believe in Resurrection,
we live at times, among the tombs of disappointment.

Let the light of Resurrection
shine into our lives today.

The Day Ahead

What am I looking forward to in the day ahead?
Who do I need to praise and thank today?
Where am I called to trust?
Where am I challenged by change?

Pause

Benedictus & Our Father *see page 4.*

Final Prayer

Let us pray for calm and clear hearts.
Lord, your presence supports us all day long.
You search out what is best within us.
Take away the fear that hides us from your sight.
Remove our blindness to your presence,
folded into the twists and turns of each day. Amen

To be repeated often during the day
The Spirit waits for us in our weakness.

Sample Pages from 'Prayers to Close My Day'

Opening Prayer

As the day ebbs away Lord,
walk with me along this evening shore.
Help me gather what the day has washed up.
Help me sift what the day gave me,
to gather what is of lasting value,
to ponder on its meaning for tomorrow.

Thinking about the Day

Offering

Lord, the tide of your love flows secretly through each day. All that this day has offered, I give to you. Let it flow back into the sea of your love. Leave me tonight with the deep peace that comes from knowing you.

Scripture

Colossians 1:15

In Jesus I see the face of God,
God who cannot be seen.
In Jesus, I see God's plan unveiled,
a plan for the entire universe forever.
Every force of nature, every human power
makes sense only in the light of Christ Jesus.
Before time began, Jesus existed.
All creation holds together in Him.
Jesus is the beginning of the Church.
He leads it each day in love.
He is the first on the journey to Resurrection.
In his wholeness we find our home.
Everything broken, unfinished and frustrated
finds completion and meaning in Him.
By the Cross and Resurrection of Jesus,
Everything is brought into place in God's plan.
Glory be to the Father,
and to the Son and to the Holy Spirit.

Scripture Reading
Hebrews 12:1

I should let go of anything that holds me back, on the journey toward Jesus. I need to persevere, despite my weakness and bad habits, in the commitment I have made to God. Try not to lose sight of Jesus. On his road, he endured many trials and setbacks. He did not give up because of shame or opposition, and neither should you. Think of Christ's journey and draw strength from the risen Lord as you travel your road.

Salesian Readings

Focus Moment

How do I feel I have worked with God's plan today?

Magnificat

Intercessions

I pray for those burdened with worry.
– May they be drawn to trust God with their future.
I pray for those consumed by anger tonight.
– May they find a new perspective in the cross of Christ.
I pray for those who have lost direction.
– May they find a guide and friend to walk with them.

Our Father

Final Prayer

Lord, stay with me this evening. As I draw this day to a close, and plan for tomorrow, sit with me awhile. Give me an eternal perspective on my choices today and tomorrow. Help me live in your goodness and enjoy the freedom of your children. I ask this through Christ Our Lord. Amen

A Blessing for Family and Friends
Let the sea of God's presence
touch their minds with peace. Amen

A selection from
Don Bosco Publications

A LENTEN SWATCH A prayer book for young people

SWATCH & PRAY A new concept prayer book for young people

SCHOOL ETHOS & CHAPLAINCY

THE CHRISTIAN TEACHER

CHRISTIAN LEADERSHIP

ORDINARY WAYS Reflections for teachers & youth leaders

TRUST THE ROAD

VIA LUCIS The Stations of the Resurrection

STARTING AGAIN FROM DON BOSCO

SERVING THE YOUNG Our Catholic Schools Today

LET YOUR HEART PRAY

LOST AND FOUND Spirituality in a changing world

A TIME FOR COMPASSION A Spirituality for Today

WITHIN & WITHOUT Renewing Religious Life

SEAN DEVEREUX - A life given for Africa

DON BOSCO'S GOSPEL WAY Reflections on Don Bosco

SYMBOLS and SPIRITUALITY reflecting on John's Gospel

MOVING ON Book of reflective poetry

MAMMA MARGARET The Life of Don Bosco's Mother

DON'T ORGANISE MY TEARS Reflections on bereavement

www.don-bosco-publications.co.uk